The NFL's Greatest Teams

PHILADELPHIA EAGLES

Big Buddy Books
An Imprint of Abdo Publishing
abdopublishing.com

Katie Lajiness

abdopublishing.com

Published by Abdo Publishing, a division of ABDO, PO Box 398166, Minneapolis, Minnesota 55439.
Copyright © 2017 by Abdo Consulting Group, Inc. International copyrights reserved in all countries. No part
of this book may be reproduced in any form without written permission from the publisher. Big Buddy Books™
is a trademark and logo of Abdo Publishing.

Printed in the United States of America, North Mankato, Minnesota.
092016
012017

Cover Photo: ASSOCIATED PRESS.
Interior Photos: AP (p. 9); ASSOCIATED PRESS (pp. 5, 7, 11, 13, 15, 17, 18, 19, 20, 21, 22, 23, 25, 27, 28, 29).

Coordinating Series Editor: Tamara L. Britton
Graphic Design: Michelle Labatt, Taylor Higgins, Jenny Christensen

Publisher's Cataloging-in-Publication Data

Names: Lajiness, Katie, author.
Title: Philadelphia Eagles / by Katie Lajiness.
Description: Minneapolis, MN : Abdo Publishing, 2017. | Series: NFL's greatest
     teams | Includes bibliographical references and index.
Identifiers: LCCN 2016944880 | ISBN 9781680785388 (lib. bdg.) |
     ISBN 9781680798982 (ebook)
Subjects: LCSH: Philadelphia Eagles (Football team)--History--Juvenile
      literature.
Classification: DDC 796.332--dc23
LC record available at http://lccn.loc.gov/2016944880

Contents

A Winning Team

The Philadelphia Eagles are a football team from Philadelphia, Pennsylvania. They have played in the National Football League (NFL) for more than 80 years.

The Eagles have had good seasons and bad. But time and again, they've proven themselves. Let's see what makes the Eagles one of the NFL's greatest teams.

Green, black, silver, and white are the team's colors.

League Play

Team Standings

The NFC and the American Football Conference (AFC) make up the NFL. Each conference has a north, south, east, and west division.

The NFL got its start in 1920. Its teams have changed over the years. Today, there are 32 teams. They make up two conferences and eight divisions.

The Eagles play in the East Division of the National Football Conference (NFC). This division also includes the Dallas Cowboys, the New York Giants, and the Washington Redskins.

The New York Giants are a major rival of the Eagles.

Fans get excited to watch the Eagles play!

Kicking Off

The Eagles were founded in 1933 by Bert Bell and Lud Wray. Like many new teams, the Eagles struggled early on. In 1941, coach Earle Neale joined the team. The Eagles started to do better. Then in 1948 and 1949 they won the NFL **championship**!

Halfback Frank Reagan (40) intercepted a pass to help the Eagles win the 1949 NFL championship.

Highlight Reel

Win or Go Home

NFL teams play 16 regular season games each year. The teams with the best records are part of the play-off games. Play-off winners move on to the conference championships. Then, conference winners face off in the Super Bowl!

During the 1950s, the team often had losing seasons. But by 1960, the Eagles were a strong team again. That year, they won their third NFL championship.

Again, the team's success did not last. It wasn't until 1978, under head coach Dick Vermeil, that the Eagles improved. Finally, in 1981, the Eagles played in their first Super Bowl. Sadly, they lost to the Oakland Raiders 27–10.

The Eagles beat the Green Bay Packers 17–13 during the 1960 NFL Championship.

Vermeil (*center*) was named NFL's Coach of the Year in 1980.

In 1999, head coach Andy Reid and quarterback Donovan McNabb joined the Eagles. They led the team to eight play-offs in ten years. In 2005, the Eagles appeared in their second Super Bowl. But, they lost to the New England Patriots 24–21.

After that, the Eagles made the play-offs several times. In 2009, they played in the NFC **championship**. But, they lost to the Arizona Cardinals 32–25. Today, the Eagles are working hard to improve.

The Eagles beat the Atlanta Falcons in the 2005 NFC championship game. The teams played in the snow.

The Eagles played the Dallas Cowboys in a 2010 play-off game. Almost 93,000 fans attended the game!

Halftime! Stat Break

Team Records

RUSHING YARDS
Career: LeSean McCoy, 6,792 yards (2009–2014)
Single Season: LeSean McCoy, 1,607 yards (2013)
PASSING YARDS
Career: Donovan McNabb, 32,873 yards (1999–2009)
Single Season: Donovan McNabb, 3,916 yards (2008)
RECEPTIONS
Career: Harold Carmichael, 589 receptions
    (1971–1983)
Single Season: Brian Westbrook, 90 receptions (2007)
ALL-TIME LEADING SCORER
David Akers, 1,323 points (1999–2010)

Famous Coaches

Earle Neale (1941–1950)
Buck Shaw (1958–1960)
Dick Vermeil (1976–1982)
Andy Reid (1999–2012)

Championships

EARLY CHAMPIONSHIP WINS:
1948, 1949, 1960
SUPER BOWL APPEARANCES:
1981, 2005
SUPER BOWL WINS:
None

Pro Football Hall of Famers & Their Years with the Eagles

Chuck Bednarik, Center/Linebacker (1949–1962)
Bert Bell, League Administrator/Owner (1933–1940)
Bob Brown, Tackle (1964–1968)
Sonny Jurgensen, Quarterback (1957–1963)
Tommy McDonald, Wide Receiver (1957–1963)
Earle Neale, Coach (1941–1950)
Pete Pihos, End (1947–1955)
Steve Van Buren, Halfback (1944–1951)
Reggie White, Defensive End (1985–1992)

Fan Fun

STADIUM: Lincoln Financial Field
LOCATION: Philadelphia, Pennsylvania
MASCOT: Swoop
NICKNAME: Birds

Coaches' Corner

Earle Neale began coaching the Eagles in 1941. He chose new players to make the team better. Neale and the improved Eagles went on to win three straight Eastern Division titles. And, they won NFL **championships** in 1948 and 1949.

Andy Reid was the Eagles head coach from 1999 to 2012. He led the team to nine winning seasons, six division titles, and one Super Bowl appearance. He holds the team's record for most wins as a head coach.

In 1948, Neale's team beat the Chicago Cardinals 7–0 in the snow.

Doug Pederson became the team's head coach in 2016.

Reid coached the Eagles to a close 2005 Super Bowl. Sadly, they lost to the New England Patriots 24–21.

Star Players

Steve Van Buren HALFBACK (1944–1951)

Steve Van Buren played with the Eagles for eight seasons. Throughout his **career**, he totaled 5,860 rushing yards and 523 receiving yards. And, he scored 464 points! Van Buren became a member of the Pro Football Hall of Fame in 1965.

Pete Pihos END (1947–1955)

Pete Pihos began playing with the team in 1947. His **career** highlights include 373 receptions and 5,619 receiving yards. Pihos caught a 31-yard touchdown pass in the 1949 NFL **championship**. He was chosen to play in six straight Pro Bowls. This is the NFL's all-star game. Pihos played his entire career with the Eagles.

Chuck Bednarik CENTER/LINEBACKER (1949–1962)

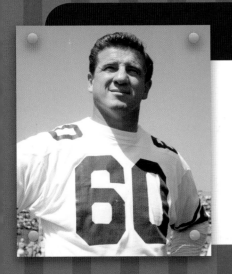

Chuck Bednarik was one of the last NFL players to play both offense and defense. He was nicknamed Concrete Charlie because he was tough. During the 1960 NFL championship, Bednarik stopped the Green Bay Packers from scoring a touchdown. The Eagles won 17–13.

Randall Cunningham QUARTERBACK (1985–1995)

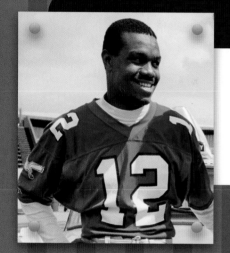

Randall Cunningham joined the Eagles in 1985 as a backup quarterback. He became the starting quarterback in 1987. A natural talent, Cunningham led the Eagles to five play-off appearances.

Brian Dawkins DEFENSIVE BACK (1996–2008)

Brian Dawkins was selected in the second round of the 1996 draft. He was a leader of the team's powerful offense. Dawkins was chosen to play in nine Pro Bowls. To honor him, the Eagles no longer use number 20.

Donovan McNabb QUARTERBACK (1999–2009)

Donovan McNabb was the first Eagles **rookie** to start as quarterback since 1991. From 2001 to 2004, McNabb led the Eagles to four straight NFC East Division **championships**. And, he helped the team make it to the 2005 Super Bowl.

Brian Westbrook RUNNING BACK (2002–2009)

The Eagles selected Brian Westbrook in the 2002 **draft**. In a 2003 game, Westbrook scored a touchdown to defeat the New York Giants 14–10. This win helped turn the team's season around. The Eagles went on to win their division and go to the NFC championship.

Lincoln Financial Field

The Eagles play home games at Lincoln Financial Field. It is in Philadelphia. The stadium opened in 2003. It can hold about 69,000 people.

In 2013, the stadium added 11,000 solar panels and 14 wind turbines.

Birds' Nest

Thousands of fans flock to Lincoln Financial Field to see the Eagles play home games. The team's **mascot** is Swoop. He wears jersey number 00. Swoop helps fans cheer on the team!

Swoop likes to be the center of attention.

Final Call

The Eagles have a long, rich history. They won three early league **championships**. And, they played in the 1981 and 2005 Super Bowls.

Even during losing seasons, true fans have stuck by them. Many believe the Philadelphia Eagles will remain one of the greatest teams in the NFL.

Jordan Matthews joined the Eagles in 2014. He loves to get the fans excited about the team.

Through the Years

1933

The Eagles play their first season.

1943

During **World War II**, the Eagles join the Pittsburgh Steelers. They are called the Phil-Pitts and the Steagles.

1948

The Eagles win their first NFL **championship**. They beat the Chicago Cardinals 7–0.

1960

The Eagles win their third NFL championship. They beat the Green Bay Packers 17–13.

1949

The team wins its second NFL championship. They beat the Los Angeles Rams 14–0.

1976

The team hires Dick Vermeil as head coach.

1981

The Eagles play in their first Super Bowl.

1978

The Eagles make it to their first play-offs in 18 years.

2002

The team makes it to the NFC **championship** for the first time in 21 years.

2005

The Eagles play in their second Super Bowl.

Postgame Recap

1. Which Eagles quarterback played in the 2005 Super Bowl?
   A. Donovan McNabb   **B**. Sonny Jurgensen   **C**. Michael Vick

2. Where do the Eagles play home games?
   A. U.S. Bank Stadium
   B. Lincoln Financial Field
   C. AT&T Stadium

3. Name 3 of the 9 Eagles in the Pro Football Hall of Fame.

4. What year was the team founded?
   A. 1933
   B. 1943
   C. 1953

Glossary

career a period of time spent in a certain job.

championship a game, a match, or a race held to find a first-place winner.

draft a system for professional sports teams to choose new players.

mascot something to bring good luck and help cheer on a team.

rookie a first-year player in a professional sport.

World War II a war fought in Europe, Asia, and Africa from 1939 to 1945.

Websites

To learn more about the NFL's Greatest Teams, visit **booklinks.abdopublishing.com**. These links are routinely monitored and updated to provide the most current information available.

Index